How to Fail at Hiking Mt. Whitney

KARL KEATING

RASSELAS
HOUSE

Published by Rasselas House
El Cajon, California
RasselasHouse.com

Cover design by James T. Egan of Bookfly Design.

ISBN: 978-1-942596-36-3

CONTENTS

PREFACE

There is no end to self-help books. No matter what your area of interest, you can find books that tell you how to succeed: how to succeed in business, how to succeed in school, how to succeed in relationships, how to succeed in baking angel food cake.

That's all fine, and many such books are useful. That particularly is true about books that help hikers hike better. You're not likely to lose your life if your angel food cake turns out unfit for human consumption, but you might lose your life if you hike foolishly in the wilderness. Self-help hiking books teach you what you need to know to have a safe, enjoyable, and thus successful hike.

Their approach is one way we learn: through direct, positive instruction. Do this, do that; follow these instructions; check off each of these bulleted points. But there's another way we learn: from mistakes made by ourselves or by others. Often, the best way to learn how to succeed at something is to learn how to fail at it—and then to avoid the things that lead to failure.

1

That's the approach taken by this book. It's not meant as a replacement for books that teach you how to succeed at hiking Mt. Whitney. There are a dozen such books in print, not to mention numerous articles and blog posts that cover the same material.

This book is meant, rather, to help you not to fail by showing you what not to do. Much of the showing is anecdotal and is taken from my own experience (I have reached the summit of Mt. Whitney multiple times—and have failed to reach the summit several times) and from the experience of others.

Even with this book there is no guarantee of success. Wilderness never makes such guarantees. The weather might conspire against you or your body might rebel against you. Most people who depart the Mt. Whitney trailhead fail to reach the summit, for these or other reasons. Some fail because of things entirely beyond their control, but many fail because of insufficient preparation, false expectations, and basic errors of judgment.

I hope these pages help you avoid the most common causes of failure. It would be a pity to get part way and realize you've made an elementary blunder that forces you to turn around. The hike to the top of the highest mountain in the contiguous 48 states is a glorious adventure. May you find yourself signing the register at the top!

INTRODUCTION

My hikes up Mt. Whitney—at 14,505 feet the tallest mountain in the 48 contiguous states—have included day hikes and overnight hikes. The former are definitely harder. No surprise there. Your pack will be lighter (no need to pack a tent or sleeping bag or several days' food) but, to use Frodo's book title, you have to go *There and Back Again* within the confines of a single day, counting from midnight. Most people start a day hike in the wee hours. As I get older, I find it prudent to start earlier and earlier, though on my first day hike of Mt. Whitney I began as early as permitted: I was on the trail as yesterday turned into today.

It was good that I left early, because I needed almost all of the 24 hours to complete the hike. It took me so long because this was only my second serious hike. The other had been up not-too-distant White Mountain the month prior.

At 14,252 feet, White Mountain is the third-highest peak in California. I thought reaching its top was the hardest physical activity I'd ever undertaken, yet that hike is easier than the hike up Mt. Whitney. The trailhead for White Mountain, which is in the White/Inyo Range above the town of Bishop on the far side of the Owens Valley from the Sierra Nevada, close to the border with Nevada, is the highest trailhead in the state at 11,680 feet. The nice thing is that you can drive right up to it on a winding gravel road that nearly any passenger vehicle can manage, though it's prudent to bring along a full-size spare tire. Most people camp at the trailhead before heading out for the summit. That's what I did.

After two miles along a service road you pass White Mountain Research Station (also known as Barcroft Station), which is run by the University of California. High-altitude physiology testing is done there. Next you pass a small observatory, and from then on it's a steady but fairly gentle walk to the top. Total elevation gain is 2,572 feet, making White Mountain the easiest fourteener in California.

It didn't seem easy to me. This was my first substantial hike. A more prudent person would have chosen a shorter trail at a lower elevation, but I had turned to backpacking so late in life that I thought I needed to play catch-up. In later years the seven miles to the top would seem not particularly daunting, but they seemed daunting at the time, so out of shape was I. Near the end, with the summit seemingly a stone's throw away, the trail mocks you by losing several hundred feet. When I got to the other side of the depression, I began to feel depressed. My legs were uncooperative. I instructed them how to move, but they answered in slow motion. Such were the effects of oxygen deprivation above 13,000 feet. I found myself pausing to catch my breath every hundred steps, then every fifty steps, then every twenty steps.

As I traversed the final switchbacks, I heard a clatter behind me. I turned to see several young people running—yes, running—up the trail as though they were running along my street back home. They passed me silently and were at the hut at the top before I turned the next switchback corner.

When, minutes later, I joined them, positioning myself on a misshapen rock that for the moment seemed the height of comfort, I asked who they were. They had no backpacks, just small packs around their waists and light jackets tied over their shoulders. They all were Canadians, in their early twenties, specially selected for participation in an experiment conducted at the research station. They were chosen for their athleticism. They had been living at the research station for three weeks and by now had become acclimatized to the thin air. Their daily task was to run the ten-mile circuit to and from the summit and then to undergo a series of physiological tests.

After a few minutes, the human guinea pigs said good-bye and took off down the trail. When they were lost to my sight, I forced myself to my feet and followed them, at a tiny fraction of their speed. It was all downhill except for that depression, which somehow had doubled in depth since I crossed it a few minutes earlier. After I reached the rise on the far side, it truly was all downhill. At length my breathing returned to normal and I was able to enjoy the scenery, which isn't at all like that of the Sierra Nevada, which could be seen far to the west.

I have never been to the northern reaches of North America, but the White Mountain landscape seemed to be like tundra, except without the bitter cold and without surface water. There were no trees and no bushes worthy of the name. There was little green at all, mainly clumps of grass. I don't recall seeing any wildflowers, but throughout my hike, coming and going, I saw—no, the proper verb is *heard*—innumerable marmots, far more per acre than I ever have seen in the Sierra Nevada.

As I walked toward the trailhead, I kept hearing squeaks. Looking out, I saw widely-spaced marmots standing on their rear legs, observing the intruder and making known their territorial claims by crying "pip-pip-pip." Wherever I turned, there were more marmots, so many that I seemed to have stumbled into a national convention of them. They were the only animals I saw. No bears in these mountains: not a berry for them to eat. No mountain lions: no deer to take down. No coyotes, so far as I could tell, unless they were adept at catching marmots before the fat rodents ducked into their holes.

So that was my first big hike, and I was unprepared for it. In terms of gear I was prepared well enough, but I was not prepared physically or mentally. There was no way I could have been prepared fully since I never had experience the effects of high-elevation hiking. I was beginning to learn that my body is so constituted that I can tell, with unerring accuracy, when I reach 13,000 feet: my legs become lead, my pace is halved. I didn't appreciate this new-found talent on that first hike up White Mountain, but I came to appreciate it after several other hikes up fourteeners—not appreciate it in the sense of liking it (I wish crossing that elevation line made no difference in my stamina) but appreciate it in the sense of unhappy acquiescence.

Back to Mt. Whitney, which I hiked a month later. It was a successful hike, and it was a failed hike.

As I said, at midnight I began the slog toward the peak, which is named after Josiah Whitney, the chief of the California Geological Survey from 1860 to 1874. For the first several hours I maneuvered by the light of a headlamp. I was making decent time, at least for someone on his second big hike. Instead of a backpack I had an oversized waist pack. Altogether, I carried 15 pounds, counting food and water. (Nowadays I would carry considerably less. I didn't yet understand, for example, that it's sufficient to carry just one liter of water because there are so many places to refill along the trail, at least up to the lower reaches of the 97 switchbacks.)

I got to the summit late morning—not a speed to boast about but not one to be ashamed about either, for a first-timer. Up to that point, the hike was a success. It soon turned into a failure. After I made the long traverse from the summit back to Trail Crest, I began to hike down the switchbacks. At some point I realized that one of my knees hurt. I hadn't stepped oddly and hadn't twisted it, but it hurt a fair amount. By the time I reached Trail Camp at the end of the switchbacks, the knee hurt a lot, and, by the time I got a few hundred feet past Trail Camp, it hurt to the point of incapacitation. It was then that I realized I should have spent a few dollars on an Ace knee brace.

I found a large, flat granite surface and laid down, my pack under my head, my bad leg cocked to minimize the discomfort. It was early afternoon, and I knew I couldn't stay much longer. I winced to my feet and started along the trail. I must have looked like the character Festus in *Gunsmoke*, swinging my now-unbendable leg in an arc, placing my foot gingerly so as not to exacerbate an already exacerbated knee. On the way up I had been making slow progress. Now I made almost no progress. I hadn't gotten very far when I realized the sun was about to disappear behind the valley wall in front of me. When it did, the shadows came on quickly, and the temperature dropped. I still had miles to go.

In my weariness and pain I thought of stepping off the trail and sleeping until the next day. That would rejuvenate my body as a whole and would allow the knee twelve hours of rest, but I dismissed the temptation when I realized that I had not only no shelter but no adequate clothing. I probably would shiver all night and not catch a wink, starting out the next morning worse than ever. I pushed on. Step, drag. Step, drag. Step, drag.

As the second midnight neared I found myself at the trailhead. What looked at the start to be an 18-hour hike turned out to take 23 hours. My sole consolation was that I got to my vehicle before my permit expired. "For the want of a nail, a kingdom was lost," runs the proverb. For the want of a knee brace, this hike was almost lost. And for want of prudence too.

Why did my knee begin to bother me on the switchbacks? Because the foot on that leg had been bothering me. I had developed a noticeable but not particularly painful blister on a toe, and I made the cardinal error: I didn't tend to it immediately. I wanted to get down to Trail Camp, where I would rest anyway, and planned to examine my foot there. That was a blunder. As little painful as the toe was, I unconsciously tried to compensate by walking slightly differently. Going down the relentless switchbacks, I had my knee in a slightly out-of-whack position, out of consideration for the toe, until finally it too started to hurt. Soon it hurt enough that the pain of the toe was inconsequential.

On later trips up Mt. Whitney, I avoided this problem. I paid attention to my feet. As soon as I noticed the least hint of a hot spot, I sat down, removed my shoe and sock, and examined my foot. Usually all I needed to do was to apply anti-friction ointment, but sometimes I wrapped a small adhesive bandage around the offending digit. A bit of duct tape would have worked as well.

I should note that on this first attempt at Mt. Whitney, as on all subsequent attempts and, really, on all subsequent backpacking trips, I took a pair of hiking poles. I began with standard-issue poles but soon graduated to super-light carbon-fiber poles that weigh only seven ounces for the pair. This means my knee problem was not a matter of clumping down too hard on my descent of the switchbacks. I always have been careful about cushioning my down climbs with poles—secondarily to save my knees, primarily because I'm a bit klutzy. I prefer to hike downhill rather than to roll downhill.

No, that Festus episode was a direct result of my not fixing my toe at Trail Crest or wherever it was that I noticed, and ignored, the first indication of a problem. I wish I could say that I learned my lesson so well that I never again ignored a hot spot on my foot, but that hasn't been the case. At least once, a few years later, I did something similar. I was leading a group hike at a much lower elevation and put off stopping to tend to my foot, not wanting to delay the others. That was a mistake. I saved ten minutes, but it cost me an hour.

By the time I examined my foot, quite a while after first noticing discomfort, I found a whopping blister that, even when drained, would admit no relief. Fortunately, we were on the final segment of the hike, but I wasn't able to keep up with the others, whom I directed to go ahead on the then-easy trail and to wait for me at a rendezvous point, where they could take their lunch. I hobbled along, far behind them, eating as I went, knowing that I'd catch up to them just as they were ready for the last leg back to the cars. As I walked I thought of an instigator during the French Revolution. He was seen running down a Paris street after the mob, calling out, "Wait for me! I am your leader!"

Aside from those incidents, on later trips I never had much of a problem with my feet, but I did have a problem with stamina. A recent one-day hike of Mt. Whitney was memorable for the finale. This was another day hike. I made decent time up the mountain but found myself going slower than usual on the downhill. I realized later that my energy stores were low; I hadn't been eating enough. This is easy to do (or should I say it's easy not to do?) because, at altitude, the body's alerting mechanisms play tricks on you, and often an empty stomach sends no signal that it's empty, just as a dehydrated system fails to let you know that your body is low on water.

This is not the case on long-distance hikes, where the body acclimatizes in a few days not just to the altitude but to the rhythm of the hike and where it returns to its normal processes, but on short but difficult hikes things seem to go awry, and you discover only after the fact that you have been hungry or thirsty or even tired for hours without having noticed it.

Anyway, on this hike the last few miles, consisting of numbing switchbacks, seemed twice as endless as they were. To save time and energy (which I had no more of) I descended to the old Mt. Whitney trailhead, which is located past Whitney Portal Store. It was dark when I reached the paved loop that marks the far end of Whitney Portal Road. I still had what seemed to be a long way to go since I had parked at the far end of the lot. In fact it wasn't far, but in my dazedness anything more than a hundred paces was far. I felt I had exhausted every calorie my body had to offer. Though I used my hiking poles even on the asphalt, I wobbled. I was gratified that no one was around to make a video of my erratic walk, which was more a slow-motion stumble than a walk.

When I got into the driver's seat, I wanted to nap, but I was too tired. I just sat there, catatonic, sipping water and thinking that I never had been so physically spent in my life. I should have downed a few energy bars four hours earlier, but, in my stupor, I hadn't been able to think in those terms. All I could think about was getting to the parking lot. I didn't ask myself why I felt so lethargic. If I had, I would have taken a break and forced down food and water.

At high altitude, as often as not, the first thing to go isn't your energy but your capacity to think. That's bad enough. What you really don't want is to fail to do sufficient thinking even before your hike begins. I hope in the remainder of this book to help you think about pitfalls to avoid.

BEATING THE PERMIT ODDS

The easiest way to fail to hike Mt. Whitney is not to hike it at all, and the easiest way to accomplish that is to fail to get a permit. Of all the trails in the Sierra Nevada, the Main Mt. Whitney Trail is far and away the most sought after. The rigorous permit system, which features a hard-to-win lottery, no doubt discourages many people from applying for a permit at all.

Decades ago, no permit was necessary. All you had to do was show up at Whitney Portal and go. The yearly tally of hikers numbered only in the low four digits. Even at the height of the hiking season—July and August—it wasn't uncommon to hike for hours without meeting anyone.

Not so in recent years. The trail has become ever more popular, and for many it has become a rite of passage. Of the thousands who set off from the trailhead each season, some are experienced hikers and backpackers, but many are first timers to high-elevation excursions. Friends tell friends of having summited the tallest peak in the contiguous states, and each year sees an increasing number of applicants for the few permits issued by Inyo National Forest.

Yes, it's possible simply to walk into the Interagency Visitor Center in Lone Pine and get a permit for the next day. Possible but unlikely. Most days there are cancellations and no-shows, even during July and August—but there aren't many. For 2014 (the most recent data available), in those months the average day saw two cancellations and eight no-shows, for a total of ten slots to be given out to those standing in line. That was for overnight permits. For day permits, the numbers were better: three cancellations and 17 no-shows, for a total of twenty.

This meant that, on average, thirty slots were available on a walk-in basis each day during the height of the season for those willing to stand in line. Slots are not make available all at the same time. At 8:00 a.m. slots opened by cancellations are available. At 11:00 a.m. the visitor center reissues permits for overnight hikes that resulted in no-shows; the new permits are for same-day entry. At 2:00 p.m. permits freed up by no-show day hikers are made available for next-day entry (that is, starting at that night's midnight).

This means there are three opportunities during the day to nab a walk-in permit. You may think that's the way to go. The problem is that many other people think the same. There may be several of them—or dozens of them—in line ahead of you. If, at 11:00 a.m., there are slots for ten overnight hikers, it's possible that the first person in line may end up with them all, if he is the leader of a group of ten. It's also possible—though highly unlikely—that each of the nine people ahead of you wants to hike solo, leaving the tenth slot for you.

If that is the long of it, this is the short of it: you take a big chance hoping for a walk-in permit. You might end up first in line—great! You just as easily might have to come back day after day, for several days, before landing a permit, or you might be shut out entirely.

That's why most people rely on the lottery. If they luck out, wonderful. If not, most of them plan to reapply the following year. The majority of those who don't get a permit through the lottery don't try to get a walk-in permit, the inconvenience being too great.

Let's talk about the lottery system. Like any lottery, you can't win if you don't play, and there are clear and simple rules for playing the Mt. Whitney lottery.

Applications are made online and are accepted from February 1 through March 15. The application fee is $6.00. You gain nothing by applying on the first day, and you lose nothing by applying on the last day. All applications are of equal status and are processed in random order. When your application is processed, if there is room on one of the dates you request, working from the top to the bottom of your list, then a reservation will be held for you. (A reservation is not the same as a permit, as we'll see.) If you want a permit for eight people and list three dates that will work for you, and if those dates have only three open slots apiece, when your application is considered, you'll end up not hiking Mt. Whitney this time around.

This suggests two obvious things: you are more likely to have your application fulfilled if you list more dates (particularly on certain days of the week—see below) and if your group is small. Your best odds are as a solo hiker: you can get a reservation if one of the dates you apply for has only a single slot left. Conversely, if you insist on having a group of ten, and if you insist on hiking the first

Saturday in August (traditionally the most sought-after entry date), then you'll have to hope that the random generator somehow brings your application to the top of the heap.

Lottery results are available in late March. Let's say you discover that you have been awarded a reservation. You can't leave it at that. If you show up at the trailhead with only a reservation, you will have shown up without a permit. In fact, what you thought was your permit will be in someone else's hand, and you'll have a sorrowful drive back home.

Your reservation is turned into a permit only if you accept the reservation. The acceptance is made online between April 1 and April 30. At that time you pay $15 per person as a reservation fee. That done, when you arrive at the Interagency Visitor Center to claim the actual permit, it will be there waiting for you.

That's the process. Now let's consider the odds of getting a permit at all. Each year the odds are getting worse because hiking Mt. Whitney is becoming ever more popular, while the number of hiking slots remains fixed.

Each day during the quota season, which runs from May 1 through October 31, the quota for overnight hiking is 60 slots and for day hiking 100 slots. This is not the number of permits but the number of people. During 2016, the average permit application sought entry for 4.7 persons for an overnight trip and 4.9 persons for a day trip. The most requested date for overnighters was Saturday, August 6, which was the first choice on 240 applications covering 1,457 people. Only four percent of those people got permits for that date. The next most requested start date for overnighters was the previous day, Friday, August 5. The odds were a little better: 1,203 people wanted to start then, and five percent of them were able to do so.

The situation was better for those wanting to go on the more taxing day trip. Again, August 6 was the most sought-after date. There were 948 hopefuls for the 100 slots, which meant a bit over ten percent of them were successful (in starting out at the trailhead—not necessarily in reaching the summit!). The next most-requested date for day hikers was Saturday, August 20: 872 people wished to head out then, but 772 ended up disappointed.

Of the ten most popular dates for overnighters, all fell on Friday or Saturday, and all but one was in July or August. For day hikers, nine of the ten most popular dates were Saturdays (the other was a Sunday): four in July, four in August, and two in September.

It doesn't take long for a pattern to emerge. This is seen most readily by glancing at a spreadsheet of applications for the first month of the quota season, May. Almost without exception, if a day's applications numbered in double digits (that is, ten or more), that day was a Friday or Saturday, for overnighters, or Saturday or Sunday, for day hikers.

The lesson here should be obvious. To minimize your chances for getting a permit, apply for a Friday or Saturday start date, if you want to spend several days on the trail, or for a Saturday or Sunday start date, if you want to hustle along and complete your hike within 24 hours. Even if you list multiple alternate start dates on your permit application, it's unlikely that you will be rewarded with a permit if you restrict yourself to weekends. You might list five different dates, but, if each one offers only a five, six, or seven percent chance of success, you'd be prudent to make alternate vacation plans.

It's understandable that people tend to choose a weekend for their bucket-list hike to 14,505 feet. For some, the best they can do is to get off work or school for only a day or two. Even for a day hike, they might have to allow for one or even two days of in-bound travel and at least one for homeward travel. But surely most people who hope to begin their hikes at the end of the week have the freedom to start a few days earlier or later. Why do they apply for the most sought-after dates? Probably because they have no idea how popular hiking Mt. Whitney is and how many people give as little thought to the calendar as they do.

We're all creatures of habit, and most of us habitually go out of town, if we go out of town at all, on the weekends. Weekdays are for work or school, except for the few weeks annually that we may be exempt from attending either one. So, on the one hand, we can say that it's understandable that a disproportionate number of people hope to start their hike of Mt. Whitney at the weekend; on the other hand, it's a pity that so few of them investigate their odds. Each year there are tens of thousands of disappointed would-be hikers. In 2016, 64 percent of the applications got this response: "Sorry, but we're full up." That's about two out of three people going away disappointed.

If it is the case—and it is—that so many of them ended up disappointed because they insisted on applying only for Friday, Saturday, or Sunday entry dates, that suggests something to those who are serious about optimizing their chances of getting a permit: apply for starting dates that fall elsewhere during the week.

July and August are, far and away, the most desired months for hiking Mt. Whitney—and with good reason. The snow that still may plague the trail in June usually is gone in July, except when the previous winter was exceptionally wet. The chilly days and possible early snows of September have not yet arrived. While the area above Trail Camp can be blustery and frosty even at the height of summer, there's a good chance, in July and August, that one can reach the summit in t-shirt and shorts (though, of course, you should carry warmer clothing just in case). Nights at Trail Camp are cold at almost any time of the year, but they seldom are shivering cold in mid-summer. Beyond that, the days are long in July and August—an important factor for day hikers who wish to minimize how many hours, at the beginning and end of their hikes, that they have to wear headlamps.

Let's look at applications, then, just for July and August. Your odds of getting a permit in May, June, September, or October are considerably higher. In the first and last of those months, you have a near certainty of getting the date you want, even if it is a Friday, Saturday, or Sunday. In July and August of 2016, the most requested start day for overnighters was Saturday. The average Saturday saw 889 applicants for 60 slots. Those applicants had less than a seven percent chance of success. Not far behind Saturday in popularity was Friday, with 786 applicants on average.

Just by avoiding either of those days, you could have doubled your chances. The next most popular start day was Thursday, with 368 applicants, then Monday with 337, and then Sunday with 308. (Sunday thus was in fifth place for overnighters but was in second place for day hikers: remember the distinction!) The next-to-last place award went to Tuesday, which had on average 258 applicants during July and August, and the last-place award went to Wednesday, with just 243 applicants.

That's fewer than a third as many applicants that Friday had and hardly more than a quarter that Saturday had.

What this means is that, all else being equal, an applicant had about four times the chance of getting a permit if he applied for a Wednesday than if he applied for a Saturday. The odds were still against him. That average Wednesday had four times as many applicants as there were slots, but that meant he had a one-in-four chance of success on a Wednesday compared to a one-in-fifteen chance on a Saturday.

If you find yourself restricted to just one particular week of hiking freedom during July or August, you would be prudent to take your chances on the Wednesday first, then the Tuesday. If your hiking week can fall anywhere during those months, then you should apply for multiple Wednesdays and Tuesdays. One could over-analyze the 2016 statistics, but, to simplify things a bit, it would be sufficient to apply first for all or most of the Wednesdays that appear in July and August and then for the Tuesdays. You are allowed to submit just one application to the lottery, but you can list up to fifteen different start dates.

You will maximize your chances of success if you restrict yourself to Wednesdays first and then Tuesdays, to the extent your schedule allows. After those, try Sundays and then Mondays. Forget about the other three days. (All this is for overnighters. I'll mentioned day hikers shortly. The advice is a little different for them.) This doesn't mean you will be guaranteed a permit. After all, taking everyone into account, nearly two-thirds of all applicants are turned down. But, if your odds are two, three, or four times better than most other applicants, you have a good chance to succeed where most fail—at the very beginning.

Now let's look at the numbers for those who want to do a day hike in July or August. Remember, a day hike is one that is to be started and completed within 24 hours, counting from midnight. The advantages of a day hike are that you don't need to carry a tent, sleeping bag, or cooking gear, nor do you need a bear canister or the many little things that are necessary for a functioning camp. This means considerably less weight on your back and considerably more speed on the trail.

The disadvantages are several. You don't have the luxury of stopping part way and getting a full night's sleep—or, probably, any sleep at all beyond a catnap. You probably will forgo warm meals (hot mac and cheese at 12,000 feet can seem far more inviting than another cold energy bar), and you almost certainly will start and end your hike in the dark.

Most people see more minuses than pluses when a day hike is compared to an overnight hike. That's why more people apply for the latter. All else being equal, this would suggest that your odds of getting a day hike permit are higher than your odds of getting an overnight permit, but things aren't equal. Your odds are even better than that, because the quota of day permits exceeds that of overnight permits.

Each day during the permit season, 100 people are allowed to enter the Whitney Zone on a day permit but only 60 on an overnight permit. This doesn't mean that only 60 out of every 160 people you will see are overnighters. Since most overnighters spend two nights on the trail—usually both nights at Trail Camp—it's as though there were 180 overnighters on the trail at any one time, compared to 100 day hikers.

But no matter. The real issue is availability of permits, and those who covet a day-hiking permit have a much better chance of securing one. Let's go through the days of the week again, for July and August, using the statistics from 2016.

Not surprisingly, Saturday is the most popular day. On average during those months, 664 people wanted one of the 100 Saturday day hiking slots. This gave them a 15 percent chance of nabbing one. Next most popular was Sunday (for overnighters, the next most popular day was Friday). The number seeking entry on Sunday dropped by more than half, to 282, giving one a 35 percent chance of getting such a permit.

Then the days went in this order: Friday, Monday, Thursday, Wednesday, and Tuesday. The last two days were nearly tied: 133 for Wednesday, 129 for Tuesday, for odds of 75 percent and 78 percent respectively. If you were to apply for two or three Wednesdays or Tuesdays, you almost certainly would be awarded a permit, with a good chance of getting your first choice.

This likelihood of success is a key reason many people (perhaps contrary to most others' expectations) apply for day permits. You can submit your entry to the lottery in February or March and feel comfortable making summer vacation plans early. Those who "need" an overnight permit for a Friday or Saturday could apply for 15 spread-out dates and still will have a less-than-even chance of getting anything at all, thus making it difficult to make early reservations in Lone Pine or elsewhere, but a day hiker can apply for a contiguous Tuesday and Wednesday with a good prospect that he will get one of them, and this allows him to snap up preferred lodging early.

GEAR TO GET AND GEAR TO FORGET

We have several outfitters in my area, one of them being REI. I've been a member of the co-op for years and frequently shop there, though more often, nowadays, for clothes than for gear. Most of my hiking gear I get from "cottage" manufacturers, small shops that may be run by just one person or by a family or, at any rate, on an independent basis. Among the shops I've used multiple times have been Ultralight Adventure Equipment (known, somewhat confusingly, as ULA), Tarptent, and Gossamer Gear. I may pick up small items at REI, such as fuel canisters and freeze-dried food, but usually I buy more substantial items, such as backpacks and tents, elsewhere.

When I visit REI in the spring, I usually notice people new to backpacking in the backpack department, trying on packs with the assistance of a store clerk. Clerks' knowledge of equipment varies, of course, as does their salesmanship, but on more than one occasion I've overheard a clerk overselling a particular pack, usually when the prospective buyer is a first-timer who proudly mentions that he has a permit for Mt. Whitney.

"This pack is bombproof," says the clerk. The customer smiles in appreciation. That's what he thinks he needs, a bombproof pack. He certainly doesn't want to find himself halfway up Mt. Whitney with a pack that has committed *hara kiri* and is spilling its contents all over the trail. I know the clerk is trying to be helpful, but in this instance his enthusiasm is getting away from him, to the disservice of the customer.

The pack indeed may be bombproof. If that's the case, then it isn't the pack the customer needs. There are no bombs along the Main Mt. Whitney Trail—or anywhere closer than the Naval Air Weapons Station at China Lake, 80 road miles away. Nor, at any point along the trail, are there protruding branches that might reach out to snag a pack, pulling it off the hiker's back and ripping it to shreds. Nor are there any obstructing bushes to be bushwhacked through. The trail, along its whole length, is free of intrusions. If a plastic shopping bag could hold your hiking gear, you could use it with reasonable confidence that at your return to the trailhead the bag still would be in serviceable condition.

The second problem with a bombproof pack is that, for many Mt. Whitney hikers, they never will be inclined to use it—or any other pack—a second time. For them the hike up Mt. Whitney will be *the* hike, their one wilderness adventure. They have no interest in repeated backpacking. They will not need a pack that will be used over many summers filled with backpacking trips long and short. They need only a pack that will get them, comfortably and securely, through a single 22-mile hike along a trail that has the same difficulty rating as a sidewalk. After that, the pack will be relegated to the closet until, years later, it occurs to them that this is one more item that can be unloaded at a garage sale or that can be donated to a charity.

The third problem with a bombproof pack is that the things that make it bombproof make it heavy. Rugged packs are made of rugged material—no longer canvas, perhaps, but thick material that adds strength while adding undesired weight. Such packs often feature multiple compartments, zippers, pockets, bungees, and straps. Is a cell phone pocket really needed on a trail that has virtually no cell reception? Wouldn't it be sufficient to store the phone deep in the pack? How many items will be bungeed or strapped to the outside, beyond a sleeping pad or tent? Two straps may be sufficient, eight straps overkill. If an internal hydration bladder is to be used, how many large external pockets are needed—and for what? If collapsible water containers will be put in external pockets, is it necessary to have an internal sleeve for a non-existent bladder?

It's easy to conclude that you should buy a five-pound pack because you "need" a pack with all these accoutrements. But you don't. I recently sold four packs that I hadn't been using much in recent years. That still left me with seven: four ultralight packs suitable for day hikes or, at best, one-night trips in mild weather and three larger packs. The larger packs are all from ULA: Catalyst (52 ounces), Circuit (42 ounces), and Ohm (26 ounces). The last of these has more than enough room for an overnighter of Mt. Whitney.

Compare the Gregory Baltoro 65 pack, one of the packs featured at REI. (I choose the Ohm and Baltoro for comparison because I own the Ohm and because, of the 150 packs offered by REI, nearly a third—45—are manufactured by Gregory. Judging from the number of online reviews, the Baltoro 65 seems to be the most popular of the Gregory packs.)

In my size (large), the Baltoro weighs 83 ounces, more than triple the weight of the Ohm, which has almost exactly the same volume. The difference in weight is 57 ounces, about three-and-a-half pounds. If you aim for a total carried weight of 24 pounds for your trip (a good target, assuming one or two nights at Trail Camp), this excess pack weight amounts to one-seventh of the total. And what do you get for it? The Baltoro comes with eight pockets in addition to the main compartment, and it has a separate compartment for the sleeping bag (something wholly unnecessary—the compartment, not the bag). It has a special pocket for a cell phone, to keep it dry, as though it wouldn't stay dry in one of the ditty bags that you'd be bringing anyway.

True, many owners attest to the Baltoro's comfort, and comfort is important in a pack. It's better to carry a heavier pack that is comfortable than a lighter pack that grinds into your shoulders. But the Ohm equally has owners attesting to its comfort. Which of the two packs would be easier on the body if you were carrying a lot of gear? Probably the Baltoro, but on a Mt. Whitney hike there is no need for a lot of gear. This is not a week-long expedition covering 100 miles of cross-country terrain.

At this writing, the Baltoro retails for $299, the Ohm for $210, making the latter lighter on the wallet as well as lighter on the back. The monetary consideration may not be important for someone who is hiking Mt. Whitney as a must-do, once-in-a-lifetime experience and for whom money is no object (and is no objection). But for others, saving three-and-a-half pounds can make the difference between a hike that is completed and one that is not.

Back to REI. Sometimes I have watched, bemused, as a first-time hiker tries on packs with the assistance of a clerk. This pack is too short, that one too long. This one has a pinching waist belt, that one lacks a sternum strap. This one doesn't have room for a bear canister, that one has room for two kitchen sinks. At length the ideal pack is found—ideal, at least, in the estimation of the clerk. It's comfortable enough, admits the customer. It's roomy, and it's even stylish. It's this year's iteration of a long-selling pack, notes the clerk, and, yes, the pack is bombproof. "Keep it on a while. Walk around the store with it. I'll come back in a few minutes," says the clerk.

A few times, feeling mischievous, I have approached the customer once the clerk has stepped away. "First time for Mt. Whitney?" The customer nods. He's heading up Mt. Whitney next month because some guys at work dragooned him into going. "Done much hiking?" None, really. "Plan to do much later?" Sure, he says, unconvincingly. "Why are you opting for such a heavy pack?" It needs to be rugged, you know. It's the wilderness, after all, not a stroll in the neighborhood park. I point out that his odds of making the summit will increase as his pack weight decreases. Why add one-sixth of the total weight for no reason? Even REI offers lighter packs of comparable size, such as the 36-ounce Granite Gear Crown V.C. 60, which retails for $199, and other vendors' packs are seen on trails even more often than are Gregory's. The customer scrunches up his nose, slips off the packs, and hefts it in his hand. "It does seem a little heavy," he admits. I walk away, my intervention complete.

I mentioned that a total pack weight of 24 pounds is not unreasonable for an overnighter of Mt. Whitney. Of course, 24 pounds would be far too much for a day hike;

one could get by with about half that weight, plus extra water needed on the final climb out of Trail Camp. But 24 pounds would be eminently doable for an overnighter, if one chooses lightweight gear and brings only what is needed. (Leave the book or Kindle at home. By the time you get to Trail Camp, set up your tent, and cook your dinner, you won't be inclined to do anything except crawl into the warmth of your sleeping bag: it's remarkable how a strenuous hike at high elevation can make 7:00 p.m. seem like the appropriate time to go to sleep.)

How much is too much? I'm a lightweight hiker, not an ultralight hiker. I have too many years on my shoulders. The greatest pack weight I can recall ever planning to carry was 39 pounds. That was for the 107-mile, no-resupply hike along the John Muir Trail from Muir Trail Ranch (the last resupply point) to Whitney Portal. That included all the food I would need for a week and considerably more gear than one would need for a one- or two-night assault of Mt. Whitney.

Thus my rule of thumb: if your Mt. Whitney pack weighs 40 pounds of more, you should turn back at the trailhead, lay out your gear on one of the picnic tables near Whitney Portal Store, and decide which ten things you'll leave in your car. Your goal: a pack weight under 30 pounds, everything included. That everything should include no more than one liter of water, up to Trail Camp. There are so many water sources along the trail that it's foolish to carry three or four liters from the trailhead. Each liter (or quart, whichever way you wish to measure) weighs about two pounds. Not carrying two liters means not carrying four pounds—an even greater savings than switching out the Baltoro 65 for the Ohm. Admittedly, you will need more than a single liter of water for the roundtrip from Trail Camp to the summit. Bring along two extra Platypus bottles for the summit attempt. You'll be leaving your tent and most of year gear at camp, so you'll still be doing the final miles carrying much less than you did at the start of your hike.

If most people carry too much water, it's equally true that most carry too much food. Perhaps they have heard stories of long-distance hikers consuming as many as 6,000 calories a day. That's the equivalent of thirty Pop-Tart pastries. And it's true that some hikers, such as those doing the Pacific Crest Trail, have needed to eat that much (though no one, so far as I know, has subsisted on thirty daily Pop-Tarts and lived to tell about it). But such extravagant metabolic needs don't come into play even in the first week of a long-distance hike. They certainly won't become apparent on a hike up Mt. Whitney. Your appetite will be pretty much what it always is, and there is no reason to pack double portions for meals. The key is to eat regularly along the trail; frequent small snacks are better than two daily gorgings.

The bywords for food are compactness and calorie density. Potato chips are great—I am willing to accept that potato chips are one of the four basic food groups—and they are high in calories, but they also are high in volume. (I discount Pringles, which, in my estimation, don't count as real potato chips, but even they are far from compact) As a practical matter—and it is important to practice practicality on a hike—you will do best with food that may not be part of your daily fare, such as traditional trail mix and energy bars, plus, for breakfast and dinner, freeze-dried food. Leave the oranges and grapes at home. Take along Pop-Tarts, but know that they will get squished in your pack. Eat plenty of carbohydrates, particularly for dinner, starting about a week before your hike; it's good to have a substantial energy store already in your body. Take one frivolous food item, something that will be your reward for each 1,000 feet you gain or each mile you traverse: a handful of M&Ms or a portion of bacon jerky, neither of which will do much for your overall calorie intake but either of which will make the slog more bearable.

Whatever food you take, if you are on an overnighter, you'll be required to use an approved bear canister. Unfortunately, eight-ounce Ursacks—bags made with Spectra fabric—are not approved for the Whitney Zone. Until such time as they are, only hard-sided canisters are on the list, and the lightest canisters are not light, coming in at not much under two pounds. If you hike with a partner, one canister will be enough for the two of you, even if you spend two nights at Trail Camp. One canister might even be enough for three. After all, your first day's food can be carried outside the canister; that food will be consumed by the time you retire for the night, which means you'll need to store in the canister at most a day-and-a-half worth of food per person (one day for a leisurely summit attempt, a half day for the hike down from Trail Camp).

One of the most unhappy ways to have a failed hike is to hike to the summit and back without problem, only to discover that a bear has broken into your vehicle, which now has broken windows, a bent door, and bear slobber all over the upholstery. This happens with surprising frequency—surprising given how often how-to-hike websites and the rangers at the Interagency Visitor Center remind Mt. Whitney hikers not to leave even the smallest trace of food in their vehicles. An Internet search for bears and cars at Whitney Portal will bring up images of cars that look like they lost the demotion derby.

Bears are active at Whitney Portal because, for dumb animals, they're smart. They know they need to fatten up for winter's hibernation. They have tried the usual routine of eating thousands of red berries. That works—bears have been prepping that way for eons—but they have discovered that people food works even better and that the pickings are easy at the trailhead. While many of the hikers are experienced backpackers, many are not, and many of the latter have little appreciation of proper food etiquette.

I remember once arriving at the trailhead, ready to head up the trail, when I looked around and saw a station wagon parked in the spot just across from where I stood. On the windshield was a brightly-colored warning tag from a ranger. The vehicle had been marked for improper food storage. It should have gotten an award for the worst food storage ever. The rear of the station wagon was stuffed with cardboard boxes. The top box was fully open, and sticking out, clearly visible, was a large, half-empty jar of peanut butter.

I shook my head, knowing that on my return three days later that station wagon, if it still was there, would be a mass of twisted metal and broken windows. The cardboard boxes would be strewn all around, and the peanut butter jar, if it could be located, would be as empty as it was when it came off the assembly line at the glass factory. I pitied the owner. He kept the station wagon in such nice shape, and now he had issued its death warrant. But somehow there was a reprieve. On my return I found the station wagon just as it was. The peanut butter was still there. So were the windows and trim and doors. So was the warning tag. All I could figure was that the bears had gone out of town on vacation.

READINESS OF MIND AND BODY

Many people underprepare for the trail. Perhaps as many overprepare. A hike up Mt. Whitney requires physical preparation, but there's no reason to fall into fanaticism about it. It's a tough hike, but it's just a hike, and it doesn't require the devotion of a prospective Olympic athlete. Consider what happens in everyday life.

Some people spend hours daily at the gym, hoping to extend their lives by a year or two. The impulse is understandable, but they fail to do a cost-benefit analysis. Forty years of devoting twenty hours weekly to workouts equals almost five years of exercising. If all that work (which may build the body but does nothing to build the mind) results in extending one's life by, say, three years, is that a good tradeoff, all else being equal? What if half as much exercise results in an extension of two years? Or if a quarter as much results in an extension of one year? Where does prudence end and fanaticism begin?

So it is with preparation for hiking. It's easy not to prepare enough. It's equally easy—and more of a temptation for many—to prepare too much. Not a few people, driven by false reports of what is demanded physically to reach the summit, work themselves so hard in the months leading up to their hikes that they exhaust themselves mentally if not physically and end up not hiking at all.

Most would-be hikers, particularly those who are out of shape (although, to be fair, round is a shape), want to drop some weight and add some stamina before reaching Whitney Portal. Fair enough—and smart enough too. Ten pounds off the waist may not be quite the same as ten pounds off the backpack, but it's close enough. You will climb the 97 switchbacks with more alacrity the more you have succeeded in countering the effects of months of potato chips and cookies.

That said, I have seen as many overweight people as ideal-weight people on the Main Mt. Whitney Trail. Admittedly, it's likely that more of the latter summited, but around the Smithsonian hut one will find many folks who never would be asked to pose for the "After" picture in an ad for a diet product.

Do you believe yourself to be overweight? Most Americans do. A Gallup poll taken a decade ago found that, on average, Americans believed themselves to be 17 pounds overweight. Let's assume that perception was accurate then and remains accurate now. A prospective Mt. Whitney hiker doesn't need to aim at dropping all 17 pounds. Dropping just a few may be enough, in two ways.

Whatever is dropped doesn't have to be hefted along 22 miles and 6,145 feet of elevation gain. Consider how much heavier your steps would be if you were consigned to carry in your hand, all the way to the top, just one standard red-clay brick. Such bricks weight over four pounds. Four of them equal those 17 pounds that most

Americans would like to drop. If you can find a way to drop the full 17 pounds, fine, but it would be enough, physiologically and psychologically, to drop even one brick's worth of fat.

For many people, the psychological effect will be more important than the physiological. If they *see* that they have gotten in shape, or at least in better shape, they likely will hike *as though* they're in better shape. Climbing Mt. Whitney is not the always-enjoyable experience of traipsing through a meadow of golden daffodils. For all the beauty along the trail, one also finds boredom, weariness, and frustration, and those are overcome better by a good attitude than by slightly-better-toned muscles.

Permit holders coming from most parts of America have no convenient way to get used to hiking at high elevations because they live at low elevations. They don't have the advantages that many Coloradans or Californians enjoy of living within an hour's drive of thin air. They will not be able to acclimatize—in the sense of getting used to oxygen deprivation—until the day or two before their arrival at Whitney Portal, but they can prepare in other ways. The main sort of preparation, of course, is to hike locally, on steep trails if they exist. Occasional hikes of a few miles, building up to those same hikes with ever-increasing weight in a daypack, will do much to get the body prepared, but it's necessary to keep in mind that every ascent, when done on the way back, is a descent.

Aside from the outbound portion of the trail between Trail Crest and the John Muir Trail junction, where one loses about 300 feet, the trail to Mt. Whitney's summit is relentlessly uphill, though it has its flat sections. (Its other downhill sections are so short as not to be worth noting.) We naturally think of going up as being particularly difficult because that is where we sweat and become winded. It is on the uphill, especially at the highest elevations, that breathing becomes difficult and we find ourselves stopping ever more frequently to catch our breath. But we need to train for the downhill too. Not to do so is to court failure.

In the introduction I mentioned my first hike (a day hike) of Mt. Whitney. Going up was grueling, and quitting more than once tempted me, but it was on the downhill that the hike turned into a near disaster, as first my foot and then my knee gave way. To the extent I had practiced for the hike, I had practiced for the uphill. It didn't occur to me to practice equally for the downhill. Different leg muscles are used on a descent, and they need to be trained equally with uphill muscles.

In my case it wasn't so much a case of muscular imbalance but of downhill imprudence. I didn't pay sufficient attention to a developing blister on my foot, and the result was a bum knee. Since I live within an easy drive of mountains that reach as high as 6,000 feet, I had plenty of opportunity to take in the ups and the downs, but I failed to do so. If you live in a state that has a high point lower than a few thousand feet, you may have no convenient access to long and steep trails—and certainly none where the air is noticeably thinner. To offset part of that disadvantage, consider using a staircase in a tall building—the taller the better, unless you live someplace such as lower Manhattan, where taller could be too tall. A staircase won't simulate a high-elevation atmosphere, but it will be an adequate stand-in for a steep trail.

Everyone has seen or heard of people who exercise by walking up dozens of flights of stairs. Perhaps even more important for the Mt. Whitney hiker is taking those stairs in the other direction. More people stumble and injure themselves going downhill than uphill, and most people's uphill muscles are better tuned than their downhill counterparts. Consider taking an elevator to the top floor of a tall building and taking a staircase to street level. Once that proves easy, start carrying a pack. Load it with two liters of water, then four, then six, to simulate some of the weight you will be lugging downward from Trail Camp. (You will be carrying little on your way to Trail Camp from the summit, having already used most of the water on the ascent from where you camped.)

Whether you hike staircases or trails, gradually increase the weight on your back. If you expect to leave Whitney Portal carrying 25 pounds, work up to carrying that much on your training hikes. When that weight feels comfortable and you find yourself effortlessly carrying it on the flats and with reasonable effort carrying it on inclines, increase the weight beyond what you will carry up the real trail. This will compensate somewhat for the effect of the Main Mount Whitney Trail's elevation. If you learn to be at ease carrying 35 pounds around home, you may have the same sense of comfort carrying 25 pounds in the thinner air above 8,360 feet.

Another reason to fill your pack (and, once the weight gets to twenty pounds or so, it should be the pack you actually will use at Mt. Whitney; before that, a smaller pack would be fine) is to learn what parts of the pack are uncomfortable. A pack tried on at an outfitter may seem as comfortable as your favorite piece of apparel, but it may feel like an instrument of torture once loaded with gear and carried hour after hour. You may discover, on your practice hikes, that you need to switch out the hip belt for a larger or smaller one or that the shoulder straps dig into your shoulders and need to be adjusted or perhaps supplemented with padding. Don't presume that a high level of fitness guarantees hiking comfort. These problems can bother lean hikers more than plump hikers because those with little fat have little cushioning.

ALTITUDE AND ATTITUDE

No backpacker ever suffered from altitude sickness in Florida. The state's high point, Britton Hill, is only 345 feet above sea level. It is the lowest state highpoint in the country. Britton Hill is located in Florida's panhandle, hard against the Alabama border. All but the tiniest sliver of Florida lies south of it, and nearly the whole of the state is as flat as the Everglades. The runner-up in lowness is Delaware's highpoint at 447 feet: still not enough to generate a sweat on an uphill walk. Twenty-eight states have no point higher than 5,000 feet, which means that altitude should not be a problem for anyone hiking within their boundaries. Thirteen states—all of them in the western part of the country—have peaks that exceed 10,000 feet.

For hikes anywhere in the majority of the states, no acclimatization is necessary. Just leave the house and head for the trail. That can be imprudent for high-elevation trails in other states. Each year Bay Area residents arrive at Whitney Portal late at night after a seven-hour drive, get a few hours of sleep, move groggily to the trailhead early the next morning, and find themselves retching long before reaching Outpost Camp (10,365 feet).

One year I had a day permit for Mt. Whitney. I decided to acclimatize by spending the previous day at Onion Valley, which is 15 air miles but 40 circuitous road miles north of Whitney Portal. Onion Valley offers a developed campground at 9,185 feet and is one of the main entryways into the High Sierra, which is reached on the Kearsarge Pass Trail. That trail gains 2,575 feet over a little less than five miles, and the pass rewards the hiker with spectacular views of distant alpine lakes and peaks.

I decided to use the Kearsarge Pass hike as a warmup for the following day's attempt at Mt. Whitney. I took it leisurely, having no reason to hurry, and was passed by as many people going up as were going down. Back at camp, I prepared a full supper and got into my sleeping bag early. I left not long after midnight for Whitney Portal and was on the Main Mt. Whitney Trail hours before sunrise. I hiked at a good pace for the first few miles, but by the time I staggered into Trail Camp—the halfway point—I realized I could go no further. I had exhausted too much of my reserve energy along the Kearsarge Pass Trail. I had felt invigorated hiking toward Mt. Whitney until my reserve stores were needed and my body discovered that there were no reserves. After a long rest at Trail Camp, I turned downhill, chastened. Perhaps I should have taken two days, not just one, for acclimatization at Onion Valley. Certainly I should not have gone to the pass, a hike that in retrospect seemed short only in comparison to the 11-mile-long (one way) Mt. Whitney trail.

On a later attempt to hike Mt. Whitney, I made good time, crossed Trail Crest, descended to the junction with the John Muir Trail, and had gone another ten minutes toward the summit when I came upon a couple. The man was kneeling next to his wife, who sat on a trailside rock, leaning toward Hitchcock Lakes, retching. They had been determined to make the summit but were two miles short. I felt sorry for the woman but wondered about the man. Why did he take her this far? She must have been feeling ill long ago and far below, perhaps becoming sick somewhere on the 97 switchbacks. Why didn't he insist that they turn around? "The mountain will be here next year," he could have said. The only cure for altitude sickness is descent. You don't get better if you go higher. You get better only if you get lower—and quickly.

I have suffered from altitude sickness only once, and then it was a mild case. It was not on the approach to Mt. Whitney but to the second-tallest peak in California, Mt. Williamson, located a few miles to the north. I had failed to become acclimatized. I knew better, but I never had had any altitude problems other than light headaches. Many people never notice anything other than the sluggishness one would expect at an oxygen-deprived altitude. It wasn't that I thought myself immune to altitude sickness. I knew full well that it can strike anyone, at any time. The young and athletic are as susceptible as the not-so-young and sedentary.

In my case, I had spent the night before the hike at the eponymously named Mt. Williamson Motel in Independence. That turned out to be a delight, because by happenstance two of the other guests recognized my name when we were checking in. They had read some of my books. We ended up having an engaging chat before I excused myself to finish organizing my gear and to turn in early.

The next morning I drove to the Shepherd Pass trailhead, elevation 6,299 feet. The motel had been at

3,930 feet, which meant sleeping there had done nothing to prepare my body for hiking high. I made Shepherd Pass in one day—many people stop two miles short, at Anvil Camp, which is the last tree-covered spot on the way to Mt. Williamson—after a gain of nearly 6,000 vertical feet. I pitched my tent, made dinner, and found I wasn't particularly hungry. That should have been a sign to me. I got into my sleeping bag early and, tired though I was, found that I couldn't fall asleep. I felt woozy. The feeling got worse as the night progressed, and I stayed ready to lean out of the tent rapidly, if the need arose.

It didn't, but by the time dawn arrived, I had slept not more than two hours. I organized my gear, put on my day pack, and started out for Mt. Tyndall, the fourteener next to Mt. Williamson, knowing it would be an easier climb. (My plan had been to hike Mt. Williamson first, then Mt. Tyndall the next day, but, given my condition, I decided to try the easier peak first.) I didn't get far. I soon realized that lack of sleep meant lack of energy, and there was no way I could climb a long ridge of talus to the summit. I returned to the tent, packed up, and went home. I no longer felt woozy—at some time during the night that sensation went away—but I no longer felt energized. I hadn't eaten much, still had little appetite, and hardly had slept. My get up and go had gotten up and gone. I knew that if I attempted to climb higher, I stood a good chance of that mild altitude sickness coming back in a more serious form, and I knew that, if that happened, I might have difficulty getting back to the tent, let alone to the trailhead.

As I said, that is the closest I've come to being laid low by altitude sickness. If, at any point along the trail, I found myself retching, as that poor woman might have been doing for an hour or more, I would have turned around. At least, unlike that couple, I knew what to do. Many people report that their symptoms dissipate after descending as little as five hundred feet. Others, with more severe cases, find they have to go all the way to the trailhead to find relief. A few never do find relief: they die on the trail. It's rare, but it happens.

It's one thing to become exhausted when hiking. That almost is to be expected. It's something else to get sick. If you were to find yourself coming down with the flu while hiking the Main Mt. Whitney Trail, you surely would head for your car and then for the nearest pharmacy or clinic. At least you would head for a comfortable place to while away your misery. Why would you head away from that and upward? If that is what you would do for the flu, which is hardly likely to kill you, why not do the same for altitude sickness, which might?

WHETHER THE WEATHER

The Main Mt. Whitney Trail is rated as a Class 1 trail, the easiest kind. This is the same rating that is assigned to a sidewalk, which may startle some people. There are no sidewalks in California above 8,000 feet (Mammoth Lakes is the highest city in the state, at 7,920 feet), so it might seem peculiar to give a trail that reaches past 14,000 feet the same rating as the concrete poured alongside the street you live on.

Trails and climbs commonly are classified according to the Yosemite Decimal System. At the top are Class 5 climbs, where specialized equipment is required. For a Class 4 trail, you likely will want to use a rope or some other sort of assistance because a fall could be lethal. In the middle is Class 3, which covers routes where scrambling on all fours is needed, at least part of the time (trails are ranked by their most difficult segment). A Class 2 trail is one along which a hiker will need to use his hands occasionally for balance or support. But the Main Mt. Whitney Trail doesn't reach even that level of difficulty. Nowhere along it must one look for handholds or grab onto rocks or branches for balance. It's like a sidewalk, but a sidewalk with steps, ruts, cobble, a few roots lower down, and, higher up, thin air.

This is both encouraging and deceptive. People of all ages, shapes, and experience have summited Mt. Whitney. That can't be said of any other fourteener in California, other than White Mountain. Heading upward, I often have passed down-hikers who succeeded in reaching the summit and yet looked, from their bulk and flabbiness, that they would have difficulty walking around the block back home.

This is not to suggest that Mt. Whitney is an easy hike. It isn't. Many people who leave the trailhead never reach the top, not because of inclement weather but because of insufficient preparation or insufficient attention to themselves or their surroundings. Some are laid low by altitude sickness. Others—as I once was—are bested by a small blister than turns into something much larger. Still others—again, I have been in their group—simply run out of energy and learn that some proverbs, such as "where there's a will, there's a way," are not always true. And then there's the weather.

One summer, after a successful summit, I was heading toward a late-morning finish, having spent two nights (one going up, one going down) at Trail Camp. I had just passed Outpost Camp and was sauntering along when I came face to face with a trail runner heading for the summit. We spoke briefly. This was his first time at Mt. Whitney. Could I estimate for him when he might top out? Based on his late start, I said he likely would be signing the trail register around 1:00 p.m. He smiled and took off.

It was a preternaturally fine day. The sky was perfectly clear, the temperature mild, the breeze gentle. I took my time on the remainder of the descent. At Whitney Portal Store I bought a much-appreciated shower. Again socially presentable, I drove down to Lone Pine and headed for a restaurant, where I had a leisurely lunch. When I stepped outside after paying for my meal, it was about four hours after I had seen the trail runner. I looked up at the mountains—but couldn't see them. A thick blanket of clouds obscured the higher elevations, coming down even below Whitney Portal.

I learned later that it was snowing hard throughout the Sierra Nevada range. The perfectly clear day had turned ominous in less time than some people take to scamper from the Smithsonian hut on the summit to Trail Camp. And scamper is just what many had to do, perhaps the trail runner among them. Unprepared hikers, wearing little more than shorts and t-shirts, stumbled into Trail Camp and begged for shelter and warmth in the tents there. These hikers not only had no proper clothing but no easy way to maneuver to lower elevations, since the trail now was obscured by snow. A bit surprisingly, no lives were lost, but certainly many once-confident hikers were humbled.

This incident occurred on September 23, but, for some reason, I no longer can remember the year. No matter. While late September marks the end of the main Mt. Whitney hiking season, what happened on that day can happen even at the height of summer. July and August have seen snow. More commonly they see thunderstorms, and this is true particularly of August, which many consider to be the prime hiking month because of its mild temperatures.

Thunderstorms can arrive as quickly as did that snowstorm, but there is a certain predictability about them too. Most thunderstorms develop in the early afternoon, though sometimes they arrive with breakfast. Look for cumulus clouds that "overdevelop" into thunderheads. When you see an anvil shape forming, prepare for a drenching. The problem isn't so much the rain, though, which may be little more than a nuisance to a hiker wearing rain gear. The main problem, or at least the most frightening problem, is lightning.

On another occasion, again having succeeded in reaching the summit, I found myself back at Trail Camp by late morning (I had left there around 5:00 a.m., heading up the switchbacks by headlamp). Just as I finished stuffing the last of my equipment into my backpack, the heavens opened up. They opened with a clap of thunder that reverberated among the surrounding peaks and seemed amplified with each echo. It is one thing to see lightning at a distance and to count the seconds before the thunder arrives. It's something else for the visual and aural components to arrive simultaneously and for the sound to come, seemingly, from all directions at once.

Trail Camp has sufficient windbreaks—large rock masses and manmade walls—to give tents some protection from Aeolus, but those rock formations offer no shelter from lightning strikes. If anything, they may be good targets for bolts seeking convenient places to connect. At 12,040 feet there is no forest cover because there is no forest. There is only the small consolation that lightning generally will strike at the highest available point—but not always.

I managed to descend to lower elevations quickly—you tend to move quickly when there is the prospect of being fricasseed—and soon found myself out of danger. I learned later that others had not been so fortunate. On the far side of Trail Crest, down in a meadow, some boy scouts had been camping. They had set up their tarps in a stand of trees, thinking that gave them the best cover possible, but the lightning was no respecter of such niceties. A bolt hit one tarp directly. An assistant scout master and one of the boys were killed, and several other scouts were injured.

Let's turn to a happier story—and an admonition about the lack of solitude.

On the first day of a leisurely backpacking trip, beginning at the Cottonwood Pass trailhead, located a few air miles south of Mt. Whitney, I came across a couple about my age. They had been in the area for several days, getting acclimatized for a Whitney hike the next day. They had a one-day permit and calculated that they had to leave the trailhead by 3:00 a.m. if they hoped to return before the light failed in early evening. The first part of their trip would be by headlamp.

They hadn't hiked Whitney before, so I gave them some tips, including information about a shortcut that would save them half a mile. They understood that they needed to be off the summit by noon if they wanted to avoid a possible thunderstorm—but bad weather seemed unlikely, given perfectly clear conditions when we spoke and a forecast that called for clear skies for the next three days.

The following day, a little after 4:00 p.m., I decided I didn't like the look of the lowering sky and that it was time to step off the trail and find a suitable place to camp. I was too late. No sooner did I have that thought than the clouds unleashed a torrent. I had to set up my tent in the rain, with my gear and my clothes getting soaked. Inside the tent I mopped up puddles as I listened to unnervingly close thunder.

I thought about that couple. If they had kept to their schedule, by the time I pitched camp they should have been halfway down from the summit, below Trail Camp. I was at about 9,000 feet, and they would have been at 11,000 feet or so; the storm would have been fiercer there. They no doubt discovered from experience what I told them at our meeting: that the trail, while an impressive engineering feat, is poorly built above Mirror Lake. Instead of canting outward, to let water flow off the trail, it cants inward, making the trail a river. There is nowhere to walk outside the trail—steep rocks on one side, drop-offs on the other—so this means you're forced to walk in ankle-deep water for a good distance: not exactly what you want to do while you're trying to scamper to a lower elevation where lightning strikes won't be such a worry.

My trip went more or less as planned, but, as is the case with most hikes, there were glitches, though nothing that didn't have a workaround. Only the one day had rain, and it lasted only a few hours (with a filigree of hail). Otherwise the skies were fine, the temperatures pleasant, and the trail spookily empty. The first day I saw that middle-aged couple. The next day I saw a lone female hiker. The third day I saw a young couple. That's an average of about one meeting per eight miles. I sought solitude, and I found it.

Certainly the middle-aged couple didn't enjoy such solitude. You can't on the Main Mt. Whitney Trail, since each day 160 people are unleashed upon it—100 day hikers and 60 overnight hikers. The trail is out and back; there are no junctions to take people out of your path, aside from a short one to Lone Pine Lake and an easy-to-miss one up North Fork Lone Pine Creek. Who goes out comes back, absent tragedy, and, if you make it to the summit and back, about 22 miles in all, you'll end up seeing most of those 160 hikers. Granted, you could see that many in an hour on many of the trails in Yosemite Valley, but the trail up Whitney still seems crowded when compared to what you usually find along Sierra Nevada trails. The last time I went over Trail Pass, which is accessed from Horseshoe Meadow (where one also finds the Cottonwood Pass trailhead and the Cottonwood Lakes trailhead), I did a long loop and saw no one for a day and a half. That just isn't possible when hiking Mt. Whitney.

NINE PRACTICALITIES

Herewith a gallimaufry of points to keep in mind. (I appreciate having a chance to use *gallimaufry* again. It's been years.)

1. Hiking is like a social event. You can underdress or overdress. Each has disadvantages.

If you underdress for a hike, you carry less than you otherwise would. If the clothing you leave behind is bulky, you save not only weight in your pack but volume, perhaps even enough volume to downsize your pack, which in turn means saving more weight. All that's good. What isn't so good is that, if the weather turns—and a clear day can turn into a thunderstorm in the time it takes to hike a mile—you risk getting soaked (if you don't have rain gear) or getting frozen (if you don't have warm clothing), neither of which is pleasant and the second of which can be deadly.

On the other hand, it makes little sense to stuff into your backpack a parka that is as bulky as your sleeping bag. Unless you hike late in the season—after the middle of September—there is scant chance that you will have any excuse to pull out anything warmer than a light down jacket or that plus a windbreaker.

All the standard Mt. Whitney guidebooks advise packing for inclement weather, though it's feasible to do that minimally if you're willing to turn around at the first sign of a storm. Few hikers take too little clothing (trail runners are an exception, but they're fast enough to scamper downhill when the raindrops begin). Many hikers take too much, burdening themselves with never-needed pounds of high-tech clothing. They find themselves running out of energy before they run out of enough warmth to warrant putting on their thick outerwear.

It bears remembering: on high-altitude hikes, where thin air makes for sluggish legs, every extra pound seems like an extra five. Add enough of those fives, and the result is a failed hike.

2. If you ought to try out the clothing you plan to take—and you should—be sure also to try out the food you plan to eat. No one does the 22-mile round-trip of Mt. Whitney on the breakfast he ate at Whitney Portal. Whether you do a day hike or an overnighter, you will take food, but will it be food you will eat? It won't only be a matter of whether you have an appetite at all (that's part of it), but will you be able to get down *this* particular meal, *this* particular snack?

Do a long, tiring hike where you live and see whether that energy bar still appeals to you. Once you return home, prepare one of the freeze-dried meals you expect to take if you'll be doing an overnighter at Mt. Whitney. (Fix whichever meal you think will least appeal to you on the trail.) Does it taste delightful, or does eating it remind you of preparing for an intrusive medical test? You will need lots of energy going up and down Mt. Whitney, but you won't be refilling your depleted stores if you take along food you're disinclined to eat.

3. Of all the foods you take with you, the most important is the one we don't usually call food: water. In theory, you can do the entire Mt. Whitney hike without eating any solid food. Your body won't be appreciative, and it would be a false economy to try to save the weight of food you really ought to be eating, but it can be done. But no one can do a 22-mile hike without drinking water. The question isn't *whether* to take water but *how much* to take. Most people take far too much, at least for the first half of the hike.

Even in drought years the higher elevations of the Sierra Nevada have copious water, and this is particularly true of the Mt. Whitney drainage. Until you reach Trail Camp at the six-mile mark (the mid-point of the hike), you never will need to carry more than a liter of water. To carry more—I've seen people schlepping five or six liters, as they hop over stream after stream—is to waste pack room and, more importantly, energy.

Water is heavy, about two pounds per liter or quart. If you carry just one liter, you carry six fewer pounds than someone who carries four liters. Those six pounds might equal a fifth or more of the other hiker's total pack weight. (It's almost a sure thing that someone who carries excess water carries excess gear. You never come across someone carrying four liters of water in an ultralight pack the remaining contents of which weigh ten pounds.) Most people find three liters sufficient for the roundtrip from Trail Camp to the summit.

The last reliable water is found at the tarn at Trail Camp, but in all but the driest years you will find water at the twenty-third of the 97 switchbacks. Many people fill their extra containers there, taking just one full one from

Trail Camp. Do note that on pre-dawn departures from Trail Camp, when nighttime temperatures have fallen low and the sun hasn't yet cast its rays on the switchbacks, the water at the twenty-third switchback may be solid rather than liquid, in which case it would be prudent to make use of the tarn.

4. I mentioned pre-dawn departures from Trail Camp. Most people depart around 5:00 a.m. Some depart earlier. They leave most of their gear in their tents or under their tarps and take only what is needed for a day hike: water, a little food, and clothing to keep warm in the hours before the sun does its work and in case cold wind or rain intrudes on the scene. An early departure means an early return. If you leave Trail Camp after sleeping in until 10:00 a.m., your afternoon approach to the summit may be obstructed by lightning and rain.

5. One thing that never should be left behind, no matter how little weight one carries for the final assault, is hiking poles. Nearly everyone hiking Mt. Whitney uses poles nowadays; the benefits to knees have been demonstrated too many times to permit naysaying. But there is another reason. Below Trail Camp the trail is reasonably well formed. Portions of it, such as above Trailside Meadow, are over granite slabs, but that is uncommon. For much of its length the trail has a respectable dirt tread. That's not the case on or above the switchbacks.

Past Trail Crest the trail consists largely of fist-sized stones. These are neither comfortable nor easy to walk on. It's easy to twist a foot, to sprain an ankle, to fall on one's face. (It's not easy to fall off the trail itself; there are two places along the final approach to the summit where there is "exposure," but that is not to be understood as being on the edge of a vertical drop, though such spots will make particularly sensitive people feel queasy if they take their eyes off the trail.)

6. The 97 switchbacks have a reputation they don't deserve. True, when covered with snow they're treacherous, but few people attempt Mt. Whitney in the snow, and those who do commonly have been to the top when the trail was bone dry. The switchbacks are no steeper than many other parts of the trail. The problem is that there are so many of them—so many that there is dispute about just how many switchbacks there are. (We will take 97 as the true number, not just because it's the number most frequently cited but because that's how many switchbacks I counted.)

The only dicey place on the switchbacks—except early or late in the season, when snow covers them—is at the cables. These begin after the forty-fifth switchback and extent not much beyond fifty feet. They perform double duty. They mark off the one section of the trail that generally will have ice until well into July, and they provide protection at the one area where a fall off the side likely would be fatal. The cables area holds ice because the uphill side isn't a slope, as along the rest of the switchbacks, but a rocky cliff, the top of which overhangs the trail, keeping the sun off it for most of the day. Repeated thawing and freezing turn whatever snow collects here into ice, most of which can be circumvented by walking on the outer edge of the trail. This is a prime area for a hike-ruining slip that ends with a fractured bone.

7. Although camping is permitted almost everywhere along the trail, for those holding an overnight permit, there are only three or four "established" camping areas, but "established" needs to be understood in the sense of

"this is where campers congregate, even though there are no facilities."

The first such campsite is at Lone Pine Lake, the spur trail to which is 2.5 miles from the trailhead. The lake is at 9,885 feet elevation. Frankly, it makes no sense to camp there unless one is planning a many-day journey up and back. For those planning to camp one night or two, Lone Pine Lake should be stricken from consideration. To do a day hike from there is not much different from doing a day hike from the trailhead.

The next campsite commonly used is Outpost Camp, which is located at the far end of Bighorn Park, 3.8 miles from the trailhead. (The distance is shorter than that, if you use the shortcuts I discuss in the shortcuts chapter.) Outpost Camp is pleasanter than the higher alternatives, having trees and a waterfall.

It's possible to make Outpost Camp one's only camp and to bag the summit from there, but doing so makes for a much longer day hike to the top since Outpost Camp is well below Trail Camp. Nevertheless, it may be the better choice for people who suspect they are not yet acclimatized. It's better to get good sleep at Outpost Camp than fitful or no sleep at Trail Camp, which is 1,680 feet higher. That may not seem like much difference, but to someone not quite in sync with the altitude, it could be determinative.

Most people camp at Trail Camp, located at the six-mile mark and at 12,040 feet. From there to the top it's nearly five miles and 2,465 feet gain, with 1,620 feet of that gain coming from the switchbacks in a bit over two miles. The chief advantage of Trail Camp is its proximity to a large tarn, where you can fetch water. The chief disadvantage is that Trail Camp can be crowded. You might consider the short hike to Consultation Lake, a larger body of water on the shores of which are several decent campsites. There you will find the privacy that eludes everyone at Trail Camp.

I said that there are three or four "established" camping areas. "Or four" refers to Mirror Lake, which is half a mile beyond and 275 feet higher than Outpost Camp. Not many people camp there, but it's worth mentioning as the last opportunity to camp within tree line.

Perhaps I should mention a fifth possibility. There is a dry bench, wide enough for several tents, after one passes Trail Crest. Easily visible from the trail, the campsite is accessed by hiking a short way down the John Muir Trail, from the junction of the Mt. Whitney trail and the JMT. It is an exposed site but is convenient for those who want a short hike—not much more than two miles—to the summit. If you think that the ten-mile roundtrip between Trail Camp and the top may be too much for one day, consider adding this spot to your itinerary. Better an extra day in the wilds than failing to reach the summit.

8. Every guidebook tells you to bring the Ten Essentials, among which is good map. For a hike up Mt. Whitney you truly ought to bring a map, but you won't need it for guidance. Aside from the spur trail to Lone Pine Lake and the earlier junction with the North Fork Lone Pine Creek trail (which is bypassed entirely if you take the first of the shortcuts I mention), there are no trail junctions until you reach the John Muir Trail on the far side of Trail Crest. Each of these junctions is well signed and unmistakable. Even in the dark it would be difficult for an inattentive person to go the wrong way at any of them, with the possible exception of the turn to Lone Pine Lake, but that short trail dead-ends at the lake, a clue that one has taken the wrong way.

The chief purpose of a map will be not to guide you to the summit but to verify how far you have come and to identify the landscape features that surround you. Be sure to use a map that includes mileages for trail sections.

Since there are no turnoffs other than the three I mention, it's almost impossible to find yourself off trail or on the wrong trail. Except for the granite slab section above Trailside Meadow, which is confusing only in darkness, the trail everywhere is clear and easily spotted. While you should take a map, which weighs nothing, you should leave home your freestanding GPS, which will be useless weight. (If you insist on taking your smartphone, download a backpacking app such as Gaia GPS.)

Even if you were to lose your paper map, you hardly could lose your way because you will come across so many others on the trail, any of whom you can turn into a guide simply by following at a distance. The route to Mt. Whitney is classified as wilderness, but you will be forgiven for thinking at times that it seems as crowded as your local mall. No one ever expired on the trail out of loneliness.

9. Let me end this chapter with things latrinal.

There once were three toilet stations along the Mt. Whitney trail. Two provided solar toilets, at Outpost Camp and Trail Camp, and the third was on the summit, not far from the Smithsonian hut. The first two were commodious commodes. There were three stalls at the upper camp and a like number at the lower, all housed in elevated structures of the latest design. The facility on the summit was more Spartan. It consisted of a seat perched on a rectangle of wood and had, on the side behind the user, a wall built from loose rocks, to screen off views from the populated area of the summit. The other sides were open to those who might be ascending from one of the climbing routes or who might be wandering away from the Smithsonian hut.

To find a higher toilet, you had to be aboard an in-flight airliner. To find privacy, you had to find somewhere else to relieve yourself. This lonely outpost (which, fortunately, I never had need to use) reminded me of the public toilet excavated at Herculaneum, which, along with the more famous Pompeii, was destroyed in an eruption of Vesuvius in A.D. 79. The Romans apparently didn't believe in toilet stalls. Perhaps it was their way of ensuring that no patron dilly-dallied.

Mt. Whitney's peak-top toilet was the first to be dismantled, as I recall. Not long after, the solar toilets at Outpost Camp and Trail Camp were removed. Park rangers said that the camp-based toilets were unable to process the ever-increasing volume of human waste. There was dispute about that. Some praised the change, saying the toilets had been inappropriate for a wilderness area. Others said that similar toilets worked without problems at similar elevations in Colorado and wondered whether there was sufficient cause to remove the ones along the Mt. Whitney trail—at least the two at the camps. (There was no general outcry to keep the toilet at the summit.) The camp toilets annually had their waste removed by helicopter—an unacceptable intrusion into the quiet of the wilderness, said some; better than toilet paper peeping out from beneath every rock, said others.

Beginning in 2007, hikers were required to make use of WAG (Waste Alleviating and Gelling) bags. One might say that this perfected the mantra "pack it in, pack it out." At first, teepee-like structures were set up where hikers could sit in privacy on a holed seat that made using WAG bags more comfortable and more discreet. After a while, those structures were removed, again on the excuse that they were not natural to the environment. Today hikers are expected to find a distant boulder behind which to take care of things.

In the early years, implementation of the WAG bag system was imperfect. Some hikers didn't use them at all. They just went off to a secluded location, much as they might in a heavily forested area. The trouble is that there is no forest at Trail Camp or even at the much lower Outpost Camp. At neither place can one dig a cat hole in the soil because there is no soil. Despite the scofflaws, most hikers made a good-faith effort to use the new system. Others made a halfhearted attempt. These latter were willing to make their deposits into the bags, but they were disinclined to carry the used bags back to the trailhead, where there is a disposal bin specifically for the bags. Such hikers left their bags on or near the trail. Sometimes good-Samaritan hikers carried out their own bags and whatever other bags they came across, but most of the removal had to be done by rangers, who may have spent more cumulative hours doing that than they ever did in their once-annual evacuation of the solar toilets.

Even with more vigorous instruction by the rangers at the Interagency Visitor Center, some people still leave used WAG bags in the higher reaches. Much blame can be laid on the fact that many hikers have no trail ethic. They perhaps never have hiked in the wilderness before and may never have heard of the Leave No Trace principle. At home, they may be used to discarding things left and right as they walk along garbage-strewn streets. People who won't carry an empty soda can to the next street-side trash bin aren't likely to carry their own waste six miles downhill from Trail Camp.

No hike ever failed because of the use, misuse, or non-use of a WAG bag, but failure comes in various forms and with multiple definitions. One can argue—and many still do—that the old system was better, if not for aesthetics at least for the environment, but the new system is the system. If more than a token number of people fail to follow it, they may not cause anyone else's hike to fail, but they do lessen everyone else's outdoor experience.

SHORTCUT SECRETS

With a round-trip distance of nearly 22 miles at high elevation, a hike to Mt. Whitney's summit is tiring at best. Many people have wondered whether there are shortcuts. There are, but only a few people know about them. The shortcuts don't reduce the elevation gain—the trailhead and the summit remain fixed points vertically, and you still have to climb the 6,145 feet between them—but you can cut the horizontal distance by more than a mile. This is significant, particularly on the descent, when your store of energy is nearly exhausted. Going down, you can save as much as an hour.

The easiest-to-find shortcut is right at the beginning. Nearly everyone begins the trail at the current trailhead, which is located just opposite the restrooms and a few yards downhill from Whitney Portal Store. The trailhead includes descriptive signboards and a not-very-accurate scale that serves no purpose other than to give poor planners reason to think that they didn't stuff too much into their backpacks.

But this is the new trailhead, which went into service in 1977. The original trailhead is located beyond Whitney Portal Store. Walk up the one-lane asphalt road, go past the store, and go to the end. Just as the road begins to curve to the left to loop back toward the pond and picnic area, look to the right. You'll see a large boulder—there's no mistaking it—on the far side of which is the old trail. The trail no longer is signed or maintained, but it remains in good condition. Just enough people use it to keep it from becoming decrepit.

This old beginning of the trail joins the main trail just above the John Muir Wilderness sign: when you get to the junction, look right to see the rear of that sign. When you step onto the main trail, get your bearings. Notice the distance to the sign, and notice that from the main trail the shortcut trail is a bit hard to see. The first few feet, looking down, seem overgrown. Keep in mind that on your return you'll be looking for this junction. If you reach the John Muir Wilderness sign, you've gone a bit too far. The junction is particularly easy to miss in the dark, which, more likely than not, is when you'll be ending your hike, particularly if you're on a one-day permit.

Apparently this beginning section of the trail proved inconvenient for pack animals because of its relative steepness. That's why the new trailhead was constructed. The new first section makes long and leisurely switchbacks to reach the junction. Ironically, pack animals later were banished from the trail, but the new trailhead remains the only trailhead known to most hikers.

Unsurprisingly, this trailhead shortcut is the easiest shortcut to find. The next shortcut is a little trickier to see on the way up but easy to spot on the way down. A couple of miles before you get to Bighorn Park, you cross a stream on a log bridge. The crossing is unmistakable. The bridge is made of half a dozen lengths of split logs. Perhaps a hundred feet after you reach the far side of the stream, look to the right. There is a steep incline that has a rock wall on the left. Follow this, keeping near the wall. The stream will be off to your right; keep away from it. You should see a use trail. If you don't, keep heading upward and move closer to the wall, at the top of which you will find the main trail. You will be a few minutes below Bighorn Park. When you're back on the trail, move ahead fifty feet and turn around to see where you came up. This is where you'll go down on the return.

This shortcut "works" because the main trail actually crosses over into another drainage, the one that includes Lone Pine Lake, making a long—and unnecessary—loop that the shortcut snips off.

When you're heading downhill, having left Bighorn Park, be ready for the trail to gain about fifteen feet. Then, when it is about to turn sharply right and up switchbacks and around boulders (this takes the trail into the next drainage), go straight and walk off the trail. You're now at the top of that wall, which, naturally enough, this time you keep on your right. So long as you head downhill, you'll run into the main trail because it passes perpendicularly to your line of travel.

Once I was descending leisurely along the main trail, not being in any rush because I had nowhere to be that day. As I neared where the trail turns right for the switchbacks, and just before I headed down the shortcut, I heard pounding behind me. I turned to see a trail runner. Moving much faster than I, he slowed only to make a breathless hello, and then he was up the switchbacks and out of sight. I immediately headed down the shortcut. When I got to the bottom, I found a trailside rock to sit on. I took off my pack, pulled out my lunch, and ostentatiously began to eat. It was several minutes before I heard the pounding again. Around the corner came the runner. When he came even with me, his eyes went wide, he smiled, and he said, both with triumph and frustration, "You know a shortcut!" And then he was off.

A third shortcut bypasses switchbacks above Trailside Meadow. It is easier to find going up than going down— the opposite of the previous shortcut. When you get to Trailside Meadow, which is really just small patches of green on either side of a stream (if you're looking for a wide meadow suitable for running horses, you're in the wrong mountain range), before starting up the switchbacks that are to your right, head instead for the upper part of the stream and cross over. Go up a short but steep rise, one you easily can see when on the other side of the stream. When you get to the top of the rise, you will spot Consultation Lake. Continue to a thin notch, and follow the notch until it joins the main trail a few hundred feet below Trail Camp. On the way back, once you leave Trail Camp, look for a spot where there are two or three good-sized campsites just off the trail to the right. These are the only such campsites you'll see in this area. Get off the trail and descend about ten feet into the notch. Turn left and keep going until you're back at Trailside Meadow.

Let me mention one last shortcut. It comes near the summit. After the trail passes the window between Mt. Whitney and Keeler Needle (the last prominent vertical point you come to before Mt. Whitney itself), the trail turns left and swoops around to the "back" side of the summit. For a good while it actually heads away from the summit. You can avoid that inconvenience by taking a hard-to-spot trail that turns sharp right from the main trail about 300 feet past the Whitney-Keeler window. This once was part of the original trail, which was rerouted to accommodate people who, by the time they reached here, had exhausted most of their energy and were disinclined (or unable) to hike steeply. The beginning of the old section indeed is steep, but then it eases up and joins the main trail. In the process it cuts off about a quarter of a mile.

Do these shortcuts make a difference? As I said, they don't save any elevation gain—you still start at the trailhead and end at the summit—but they eliminate a fair amount of the horizontal, perhaps about a mile's worth. That may seem a small amount when you're hiking on fairly level ground at your home's elevation. It can mean the difference between success and failure when trying to climb Mt. Whitney. Not only do the shortcuts reduce length; they reduce time. On the descent, they can save you about an hour. When your body is as exhausted as it ever has been and you're wondering whether you have the energy to get back to your car, saving an hour can mean saving the hike.

And now an encouraging word for older hikers.

Robert Rockwell is one of the best known Mt. Whitney denizens. He was 16 when he first summited (wearing street shoes, of all things). That was in 1952. In the years since he climbed more than 1,700 peaks around the world and got to Mt. Whitney's top more than 150 times. In 1999 he wrote a humorous account of making good use of these and other shortcuts. The piece was titled "Old Age and Trickery." Rockwell was 63 at the time.

He had planned to make use of four shortcuts on this particular trip. When he got out of his car, he found himself next to five men about half his age. They were from a Lake Tahoe runners' club. They said they wanted to get up and back quickly, and Rockwell offered to hike with them, saying he could show them shortcuts. They politely declined his offer. It was obvious to Rockwell that they imagined he would be a burden and not a help.

They headed off at the current trailhead, and Rockwell made his way to the old trailhead. He got to the junction with the main trail, near the John Muir Wilderness sign, and could hear the other five at a distance. He was surprised at their speed, but they were running, which is what trail runners do. He dropped his packed, walked down the trail in their direction, to fill his canteen at a stream, and sat down for a drink. By the time they reached him they were walking. He said they looked surprised and said nothing more than hello.

Rockwell followed them a short way and then took his second shortcut—one I don't mention in this book because it's hard to find. When he topped out, he sat down, starting munching on a sandwich, and waited. Ten minutes later the first of the five reached him and said, "Nice shortcuts." Within a few minutes the others passed by.

Then Rockwell crossed the wide stream with the cut-log bridge and went up the shortcut described earlier, ending below Bighorn Park. He walked part of the way toward Outpost Camp, sat down by a spring, and took another drink. The five walked past him, slowly: he bemused and they not amused.

Rockwell followed along the main trail. When he reached Trailside Meadow, keeping them in view ahead of him, he cut left as they headed to the right and up the long switchbacks. When he got to Trail Camp, the five weren't anywhere to be seen. Thinking they were ahead of him, Rockwell headed up the 97 switchbacks. After gaining about 400 feet, he looked back to see the others just entering Trail Camp.

At the top of the switchbacks is Trail Crest at 13,600 feet. Here two of the others passed him. The other three Rockwell wouldn't see again. He followed the two toward the summit, managing to keep a constant distance behind them because they had exhausted much of their store of energy—the penalty for running at the start.

After passing Keeler Needle, and seeing that the two had stayed on the main trail and were making the wide swing to the left, Rockwell took his last shortcut. He reached the hut at the summit, waited for fifteen minutes, and then headed down, never seeing the hikers again. Presumably the two staggered to the hut shortly after he departed; the other three likely did not make the summit at all, since Rockwell didn't see them on his way down. They may have turned around at Trail Camp.

In any case, the shortcuts saved Rockwell enough distance, time, and energy that he was able to do the round trip in hardly more than ten hours—a very good rate for anyone of any age.

PARTING THOUGHTS

More people fail at hiking Mt. Whitney than fail at hiking any other Sierra Nevada route. Partly that's because Mt. Whitney attracts so many inexperienced hikers, but experienced hikers also fail to reach the summit—or even fail to nab a permit. Some who have been backpacking for years on shorter, lower, or less steep trails become complacent, particularly when they hear that so many first-time hikers succeed. ("If *they* can reach the top, it'll be a cinch for me.")

As I wrote at the beginning, there is no guarantee of a successful Mt. Whitney hike. While some things are beyond your control, such as whether your application will be considered early in the lottery or at the end, there are things you can do to improve your chances at every stage of the process.

At the application stage, you can apply for Tuesdays and Wednesdays rather than for Fridays and Saturdays. At the preparation stage, you can ready yourself intelligently, neither underpreparing nor overpreparing, and you can choose the right gear and the right amount of gear. At the execution stage, you can make allowances for altitude and weather before they overpower you, and you can save time and energy by taking trail shortcuts.

Each year, thousands of hikers sign the trail register at the top of Mt. Whitney. Each year, thousands of others bungle their chances and never reach the top. There's no reason you should be in the second group.

I hope these pages, by showing you how to fail, help you too to reach 14,505 feet.

ABOUT THE AUTHOR

Karl Keating has written fifteen books. For three decades he has worked as an editor and publisher. He holds advanced degrees in theology and law plus an honorary doctor of laws degree. His avocations include hiking, studying languages, and playing the baroque mandolino. You can follow him at his author website and at his Facebook page:

KarlKeating.com

Facebook.com/KarlKeatingBooks

Made in the USA
Las Vegas, NV
11 December 2023

82526610R00046